I0816508

GROUNDBREAKER BIOS

Jackie Robinson

BY HEATHER C. HUDAK

CONTENT CONSULTANT
RANDY ROBERTS, PhD
DISTINGUISHED PROFESSOR OF HISTORY
PURDUE UNIVERSITY

Kids Core
An Imprint of Abdo Publishing
abdobooks.com

abdobooks.com

Published by Abdo Publishing, a division of ABDO, PO Box 398166, Minneapolis, Minnesota 55439.

Printed in the United States of America, North Mankato, Minnesota.
102021
012022

Cover Photo: DG/AP Images
Interior Photos: Bettmann/Getty Images, 4–5, 10–11, 12, 28; Hulton Archive/Getty Images, 6; iStockphoto, 8; PhotoQuest/Archive Photos/Getty Images, 15; Globe Photos/Zuma Press/Alamy, 16; Shutterstock Images, 17 (baseball); David Durochik/AP Images, 18; Transcendental Graphics/Getty Images Sport/Getty Images, 20–21; Tim Roske/AP Images, 22, 29 (bottom); RBM Vintage Images/Alamy, 24; Alex Gallardo/AP Images, 26, 29 (top)

Editor: Ann Schwab
Series Designer: Christine Ha

Library of Congress Control Number: 2021941508

Publisher's Cataloging-in-Publication Data

Names: Hudak, Heather C., author.
Title: Jackie Robinson / by Heather C. Hudak
Description: Minneapolis, Minnesota : Abdo Publishing, 2022 | Series: Groundbreaker bios | Includes online resources and index.
Identifiers: ISBN 9781532196867 (lib. bdg.) | ISBN 9781644946701 (pbk.) | ISBN 9781098218676 (ebook)
Subjects: LCSH: Robinson, Jackie, 1919-1972--Juvenile literature. | Baseball players--Biography--Juvenile literature. | Brooklyn Dodgers (Baseball team)--Juvenile literature. | African American baseball players--Biography--Juvenile literature. | Negro leagues--Juvenile literature. | Civil rights workers--Biography--Juvenile literature.
Classification: DDC 796.357092 [B]--dc23

CONTENTS

Jackie Robinson had a Hall of Fame career.

CHAPTER 1

Who Was Jackie Robinson?

Jackie Robinson stepped onto Ebbets Field in New York City, wearing his Brooklyn Dodgers uniform. The date was April 15, 1947. That day he became the first Black player in Major League Baseball (MLB) since the 1800s.

Jackie, *second from left*, with his family when he was about six years old

Many white fans refused to come to the game. He could hear some people boo.

At the time, many white people did not treat Black people as equals. Robinson worried that his teammates and other players in the league might not accept him. But that didn't stop him from playing his best. That day was the beginning of his remarkable career. He played so well that season that he was named Rookie of the Year. People began to see him as a talented athlete instead of seeing only the color of his skin. Even more important, that April day in 1947 marked a turning point for Black Americans.

What Is Segregation?

Segregation is the act of keeping people apart from each other based on race. It was legal in the United States until the mid-1900s. Black people did not have the same rights as white people. They were treated unfairly because of their skin color. Black people were kept separate from white people in schools, hospitals, buses, and many other places. In some ways, segregation still exists.

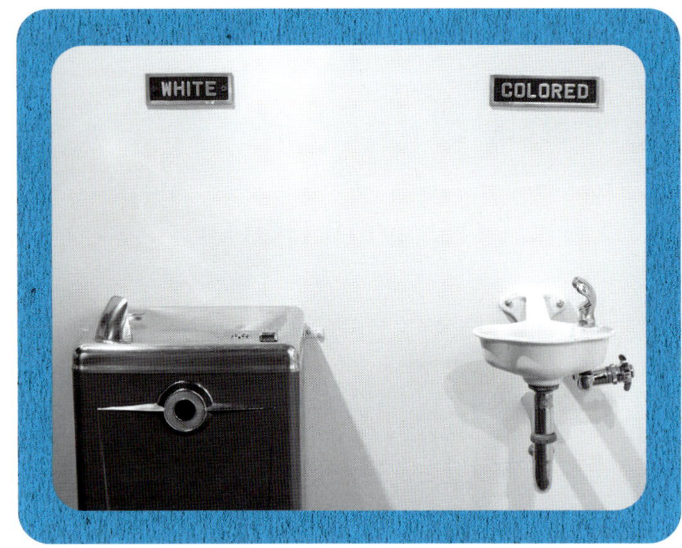

In many places before 1964, Black people were not allowed to drink from the same drinking fountains as white people.

Jackie's Early Years

Jack Roosevelt Robinson was born on January 31, 1919, in Cairo, Georgia. He was the youngest of five children born to Jerry and Mallie Robinson. Jackie's father left in 1920. Mallie then moved the family to Pasadena, California.

Jackie was a star athlete even as a teen. People cheered for him on the field. But off the field, many people treated him unfairly because he was Black.

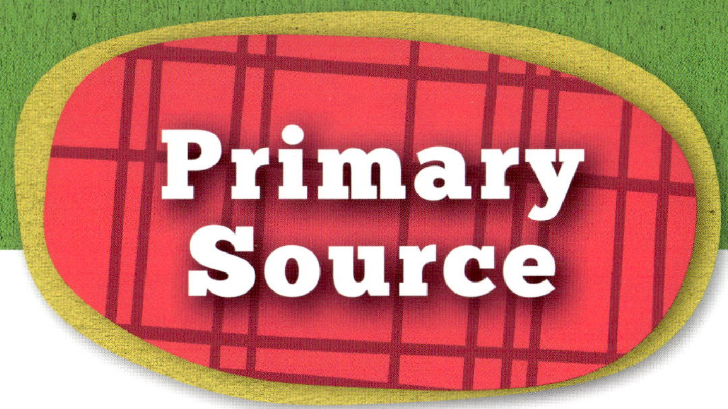

Robinson talked about how he felt at his first game with the Montreal Royals, the **farm team** for the Dodgers:

> I stood on the baseline with a lump in my throat and my heart beating rapidly, my stomach feeling as if it were full of feverish fireflies with claws on their feet.

Source: Carl T. Rowan and Jackie Robinson. *Wait Till Next Year: The Life Story of Jackie Robinson*. Random House, 1960.

What's the Big Idea?

Read this quote carefully. What is its main idea? Explain how the main idea is supported by details.

Jackie Robinson was a star in four sports at UCLA, including football.

CHAPTER 2

Journey to the Big Leagues

Robinson went to Pasadena Junior College in 1937. In 1939, he started school at the University of California, Los Angeles (UCLA). He was the first UCLA athlete to letter in four sports in the same year. This is an award an athlete receives when he or she excels in a sport.

Robinson was a Second Lieutenant in the US Army during World War II (1939–1945).

No one has been able to do it since. But he could not afford to finish school. He left in 1941.

Robinson was **drafted** into the US Army in 1942. There, he began standing up for **civil rights**. In 1944, Robinson was riding on a bus. The bus driver told him to go to the back of the bus. That is where Black people were forced to sit, except on military buses. Robinson refused, and the military police arrested him. He was put on trial, but he was found not guilty.

Civil Rights

The civil rights movement of the 1950s and 1960s was a struggle for social justice. It called for equal rights for Black people. Robinson was a civil rights **activist**.

He left the army on good terms in 1944. Robinson started playing shortstop for the Kansas City Monarchs soon after. They were part of a baseball league for Black players. Many sports were segregated at the time.

In 1945, Robinson signed on to play for the Brooklyn Dodgers. First, he spent a year playing with the Montreal Royals. They were the Dodgers' farm team.

Meanwhile, Robinson married Rachel Isum in February 1946. They had met at UCLA. The couple went on to have three children: Jack Jr., Sharon, and David.

Once Robinson began playing for the Dodgers in 1947, he quickly became a star.

Jackie and Rachel Robinson with young Jack Jr.

Robinson stole home base an incredible 19 times during his career.

In 1949, he was named the National League's Most Valuable Player. He played in six All-Star Games. Robinson and his team went to the World Series six times. They became champions in 1955.

Many people were **racist** toward Robinson. He even received death threats. But Robinson stayed focused on the game.

Jackie Robinson's Hall of Fame Stats

- .313 Batting Average
- 4,997 At-Bats
- 1,563 Career Hits
- 972 Runs
- 141 Home Runs
- 200 Stolen Bases
- 1,416 Games Played

Jackie Robinson was one of the greatest baseball players of all time. These are his statistics over his ten-year career.

Other Black players soon joined Robinson in the American and National Leagues, including fellow superstar Willie Mays.

Robinson's success allowed other Black athletes to play baseball alongside white players. It also made a big impact outside of baseball. People saw how Robinson played with skill and was calm under pressure. They noticed how his teammates and fans accepted him. More white people began to believe segregation was wrong. Society began to change. One year later, segregation was no longer allowed in the military. A few years later, segregation was no longer permitted in public schools.

Further Evidence

Look at the website below. Does it give any new evidence to support Chapter Two?

Jackie Robinson

abdocorelibrary.com/jackie-robinson-bio

After retiring from baseball, Robinson became a business executive.

CHAPTER 3

Civil Rights Work and Legacy

Robinson retired from baseball in 1957. He wanted to manage or coach in the major leagues but didn't get any offers. It would be 17 more years before there was a Black manager in MLB.

Robinson was named vice president of Chock Full o' Nuts.

Jackie Robinson's plaque at the National Baseball Hall of Fame

That made him the first Black person to be a vice president of a major American business.

He also cofounded the Freedom National Bank. Its goal was to serve Black customers in the Harlem area of New York City. Robinson wrote many books and hosted a radio show. He even starred in a movie about his life. On July 23, 1962, Robinson became the first Black player **inducted** into the National Baseball Hall of Fame.

Robinson also continued his civil rights work. In fact, he was on the board of the National Association for the Advancement of Colored People (NAACP). This organization works to gain equal rights for Black people. It fights against unfair treatment of them.

Robinson and his son David attended the March on Washington in 1963 to support civil rights.

Robinson asked US presidents to support civil rights. He gave speeches, took part in marches, and wrote newspaper columns. Robinson died of a heart attack on October 24, 1972.

Robinson had many accomplishments on and off the field. He broke down the color barrier in baseball, paving the way for other Black athletes. He fought for equal rights for Black Americans. To honor his life's work, he was awarded the Presidential Medal of Freedom by then-president Ronald Reagan in 1984.

Jackie Robinson Foundation

Robinson's wife formed the Jackie Robinson Foundation soon after his death. The foundation helps minority students pay for college.

Every MLB player wears number 42 on April 15 to honor Jackie Robinson.

The 1997 MLB season was played in honor of Robinson's first game 50 years earlier. MLB also retired his number 42 jersey that year. He is the only player to be honored this way in any sport. Each year on April 15, MLB celebrates Jackie Robinson Day. All players wear Robinson's number on that day. The entire league remembers and honors his lasting legacy.

Explore Online

Visit the website below. Does it give any new information about Jackie Robinson Day that wasn't in Chapter Three?

Jackie Robinson Day

abdocorelibrary.com/jackie-robinson-bio

Timeline

1919
Jackie Robinson is born in Cairo, Georgia, on January 31.

1944
Robinson stands up for his civil rights while serving in the US Army.

1947
On April 15, Robinson plays his first Major League Baseball game with the Brooklyn Dodgers.

1962

On July 23, Robinson becomes the first Black player inducted into the National Baseball Hall of Fame.

1997

On April 15, Robinson becomes the only player in Major League Baseball history to have his number retired by every team.

1972

Robinson dies of a heart attack on October 24.

Glossary

activist
a person who believes strongly in a cause and takes action to achieve specific goals

civil rights
the rights of all people to be treated equally

drafted
to be selected for some purpose

farm team
a minor league baseball team that is associated with a major league baseball team

inducted
admitted as a member into a special group

racist
reflecting a false belief that some people are worse or inferior because of their race

segregation
the act of keeping people apart from each other based on race

Online Resources

To learn more about Jackie Robinson, visit our free resource websites below.

Visit **abdocorelibrary.com** or scan this QR code for free Common Core resources for teachers and students, including vetted activities, multimedia, and booklinks, for deeper subject comprehension.

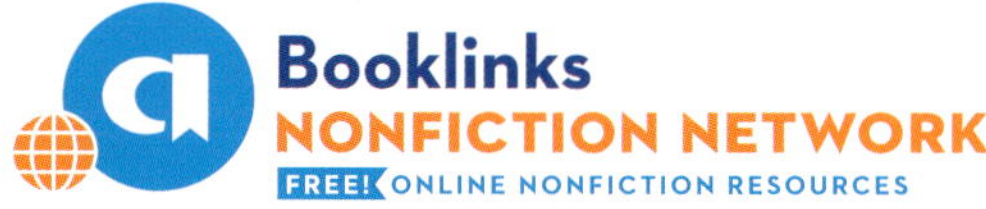

Visit **abdobooklinks.com** or scan this QR code for free additional online weblinks for further learning. These links are routinely monitored and updated to provide the most current information available.

Learn More

Rappaport, Doreen. *42 Is Not Just a Number: The Odyssey of Jackie Robinson, American Hero.* Candlewick, 2017.

Smith, Sherri L. *What Is the Civil Rights Movement?* Penguin Workshop, 2020.

Index

About the Author

Heather C. Hudak has written hundreds of kids' books on all kinds of topics. She loves to travel when she's not writing. Heather has visited about 60 countries. One of her favorite places to visit is the state of California, where Jackie Robinson grew up.